The Woman
Who Died
in Her Sleep

POETRY BY
LINDA GREGERSON

Fire in the Conservatory

The Woman Who Died in Her Sleep

The Woman
Who Died
in Her Sleep

LINDA GREGERSON

A Mariner Book
Houghton Mifflin Company   Boston   New York

For information about permission to reproduce selections from this book,
write to Permissions, Houghton Mifflin Company, 215 Park Avenue South,
New York, New York 10003.

Library of Congress Cataloging-in-Publication Data
Gregerson, Linda.
 The woman who died in her sleep / Linda Gregerson.
   p.   cm.
 Poems.
 ISBN 0-395-82290-4   ISBN 0-395-82289-0 (pbk.)
 I. Title
PS3557.R425W6   1996
811'.54 — dc20   96-21179   CIP

Printed in the United States of America

QUM 10 9 8 7 6 5 4 3 2 1

Acknowledgments

Grateful acknowledgment to the editors of the following publications, in which these poems
first apppeared:
 The Atlantic Monthly: "The Bad Physician," "For the Taking," "Mother Ruin," "Safe,"
"Target." *The Boston Review:* "Sold." *Colorado Review:* "Creation Myth," "Salt." *Grand
Street:* "Saints' Logic." *Kenyon Review:* "With Emma at the Ladies-Only Swimming Pond on
Hampstead Heath," "Luke 17:32." *Partisan Review:* "For My Father, Who Would Rather Stay
Home," "Bad Blood." *Ploughshares:* "Fish Dying on the Third Floor at Barneys." *Poetry:*
"An Arbor," "Good News," "The Resurrection of the Body," "Bleedthrough." *Triquarterly:*
"Bunting." *The Yale Review:* "The Woman Who Died in Her Sleep."
 "Safe" was reprinted in *The Best American Poetry 1991,* Mark Strand, ed., David Lehman,
series ed. (New York: Scribners and Macmillan/Collier, 1991).
 "An Arbor" and "Good News" were awarded the Levinson Prize by *Poetry* in 1991.
 "For the Taking" received the 1992 Consuelo Ford Award from the Poetry Society of
America and was reprinted in *PSA News* (Newsletter of the Poetry Society of America) 43
(Winter 1994). It was subsequently reprinted in *Nature's Ban: Women's Incest Literature,* Karen
Jacobsen McLennan, ed. (Boston: Northeastern University Press, 1996).
 "Salt" was reprinted in *The Pushcart Prize Anthology* 19 (1994), Bill Henderson, ed., Lynn
Emanuel and David St. John, poetry eds.
 "Good News" and "Saints' Logic" were reprinted in *The Boston Review.*
 "An Arbor" was reprinted in *Orion.*
 "Creation Myth" was reprinted in *The University of Iowa Museum of Art Anniversary An-
thology,* Jorie Graham and Kim Merker, eds. (Iowa City: Windhover Press, 1996).
 "Line Drive Caught by the Grace of God" originally appeared in *Fire in the Conservatory*
(Port Townsend, Wash.: Dragon Gate Press, 1982).

I would also like to thank the National Endowment for the Arts, the National Humanities
Center, the Arts Foundation of Michigan, and the University of Michigan for grants that en-
abled me to complete this book.

FOR EMMA

AND FOR MEGAN

Contents

The source tale is slightly different: when the third daughter is asked to win her share of the kingdom by declaring her love for her father the king, she says, "I love you more than salt."

The Woman
Who Died
in Her Sleep

The Bad Physician

The body in health, the body in sickness,
            inscribing
        its versatile logic till the least

of us must, willy-nilly, learn
                to read.
            And even in error, as when

the mutant multiplies, or first
                my right eye,
            now my left, is targeted

for harm by the system
                designed
            to keep it safe,

even in error the body
                wields cunning
            as birches in leaf wield light.

The child who swallows the amnion now
                will swallow milk
            by winter. The milk

can find a use for me but not
                for my belief,
            nor yours, and it beggars the best

of our purposes. Within us
                without us,
            this life is already beyond us,

so what must it make of the man who cures
                by rote?
            My friend's young daughter moved

with a slightly muddied
                gait,
            and then her tongue

and then her hands
                unlearned
            their freedom, so newly

acquired. Unlearned with great
                labor
            while the tumor thrived,

and all the elixirs in Mexico
                could not
            revise her sentence by a day.

You who make your living at
                the body's re-
            versible deviations,

what will you say to a six-
                year-old
            when all her bright first lessons

are defaced? Even the skeptic
                in his lab,
        who works at the friable boundaries

of our common
                legibility
        and does the work that I trust

best, is bound to frame his question
                in the pure,
        distorting light of hope.

The beautiful cells dividing have
                no mind
        for us, but look

what a ravishing mind
                they make
        and what a heart we've nursed

in its shade, who love
                that most
        which leaves us most behind.

For My Father, Who Would
Rather Stay Home

No deadfall in these woods of yours.
>   No
>   hollowed-out trunks.

No needy,
>   unseemly
>   hanging on, as puts

a man with a chainsaw
>   to shame.
>   The row of rusting oildrums and the

spavined Ford are nearly
>   obscured
>   by sumac and scrub,

whose thin-legged plans for the future
>   outrun
>   all reasonable grounds for hope.

It's ground you never meant
>   to give.
>   If bracken

wants to euphemize an un-
>   regenerate
>   combine and a heap

of salvaged pipe,
                    it works
            its homely camouflage unbidden

and unblessed.
                    The Ford
            might lend you parts someday, and woe

betide the nesting squirrels
                    who've taken
            to its deep front end. Life

is exactly long
                    enough,
            except for the thin-skinned

or beggarly
                    daughters,
            who haven't struck your bargain

with the pure hard edge
                    of luck.
            Remember when we planted the Norway

pine? Five hundred seedlings
                    the first
            year and not one of them made

full growth. No light.
                    Or scant
            light, what the grudging oaks

let through. What you love
                best
        shall be taken away

and taken away in the other
                life too,
        where you haven't got

a stand of oak at all,
                old man,
        nor three winters' cordwood,

nor work for the heart,
                nor hapless
        daughters

to mortgage everything up.
                You think
        I haven't gathered how

the world divides?
                The un-
        stanched, unrequited lapse

of time has been your
                quarrel
        since before I learned to

temporize, till every other
                word's
        goodbye. It shouldn't be

too much to ask, this
                dying
        on familiar ground, but look

at the bracken, keeping
                the ground
        in place. You who don't

reproach me
                reproach me
        with failing to see,

as though a traveler,
                finding
        the inn a pleasant one,

should lose his way.
                The way
        you have in mind makes mine

digression, but
                while age
        may be your privilege, it's

no alibi.
                The parable
        means absent without leave,

you see. I'll keep you
                as long
        as the woods are deep,

and then I'll let you go.

Saints' Logic

Love the drill, confound the dentist.
Love the fever that carries me home.
Meat of exile. Salt of grief.
This much, indifferent

affliction might yield. But how
when the table is God's own board
and grace must be said in company?
If hatred were honey, as even

the psalmist persuaded himself,
then Agatha might be holding
her breasts on the plate for reproach.
The plate is decidedly

ornamental, and who shall say that pity's
not, at this remove? Her gown
would be stiff with embroidery whatever
the shape of the body beneath.

Perhaps in heaven God can't hide
his face. So the wounded
are given these gowns to wear
and duties that teach them the leverage

of pain. Agatha listens with special
regard to the barren, the dry,
to those with tumors where milk
should be, to those who nurse

for hire. Let me swell,
let me not swell. Remember the child,
how its fingers go blind as it sucks.
Bartholomew, flayed, intervenes

for the tanners. Catherine for millers,
whose wheels are of stone. Sebastian
protects the arrowsmiths, and John
the chandlers, because he was boiled

in oil. We borrow our light
where we can, here's begging the pardon
of tallow and wick. And if, as we've tried
to extract from the prospect, we'll each

have a sign to be known by at last —
a knife, a floursack, a hammer, a pot —
the saints can stay,
the earth won't entirely have given us up.

Safe

K.M.S. 1948–1986

I.

The tendons sewn together and the small bones
   healed, that your hand
  might close on a pencil again

or hold a cup. The delicate muscles made
   whole again,
  to lift your eyelid and govern your smile,

and the nerves new-laid in their tracks.
   The broken
  point of the kitchen knife — and here

let the surgeon be gentle — removed and the skull
   knit closed
  and the blood lifted out of the carpet and washed

from the stairs. And the nineteen-year-old burglar returned
   to the cradle or
  his mother's arms, he must have been harmless

once, even he, who is not sorry, had
   nothing
  to lose, and will never be harmless again.

2.

Emma is learning to wield her own spoon —
        silver for abundance,
      though it seldom finds her mouth as yet.

She hates to be fed, would rather starve,
        but loves
      to steer the precarious course herself.

Silver for pride, then, or luck of the sort
        some children
      are born with, omitting

the manifold slippage
        that separates
      privilege and weal. Luck in this popular figure

is three parts silver anyway,
        that the child
      not succumb to crack in the schoolyard,

rats in the hall, the clever fence with a
        shopping list,
      bad plumbing, bad food, and hatred-on-a-staircase

with a knife in hand and dim designs
        on jewelry
      or a VCR. The spoon was superfluity —

the best part of your paycheck for a child
                you haven't lived
            to see. Friend, her cheek is fresh as hope

of paradise. And every passing minute in the hours
                of light
            and the hours of darkness, in the fever

of pneumonia or the ignorant sweet wash
                of health,
            the miraculous breath

moves into her lungs and, stitch
                by mortal
            stitch, moves out.

                        3.

When the paramedics came at last, my friend
                apologized:
            she must have hit her head, she thought,

she'd just take a minute to mop up the mess
                by the phone.
            Her broken hands, for which

the flaw in memory had provided no such
                alibi,
            her broken hands had kept him two or

three times from her face.
> And later,
>   when the anesthesiologist had

launched her on his good green gas
> and launched her,
>   as they do sometimes, a shade too fast,

she slipped the bonds of recall altogether.
> Safe
>   as houses. You know what a house is for the likes

of us: downpayment on the nursing home,
>   our foursquare
>   pledge to be debtors of conscience, if debtors

in conscience may not look too closely
>   where credit's
>   refused. Our piece of the here for here-

after, which shows us diminished regard
>   and just
>   such a face as fear has made:

one night a woman came home to her house
>   and locked its useless
>   locks, and buttoned her nightdress and read

for a while, and slept till she was wakened.

An Arbor

1.

The world's a world of trouble, your mother must
        have told you
          that. Poison leaks into the basements

and tedium into the schools. The oak
        is going the way
          of the elm in the upper Midwest — my cousin

earns a living by taking the dead ones
        down.
        And Jason's alive yet, the fair-

haired child, his metal crib next
        to my daughter's.
        Jason is nearly one year old but last

saw light five months ago and won't
        see light again.

2.

Leaf against leaf without malice
        or forethought,
        the manifold species of murmuring

harm. No harm intended, there never is.
                    The new
            inadequate software gets the reference librarian

fired. The maintenance crew turns off power one
                    weekend
            and Monday the lab is a morgue: fifty-four

rabbits and seventeen months of research.
                    Ignorance loves
            as ignorance does and always

holds high office.

                    3.

Jason had the misfortune to suffer misfortune
                    the third
            of July. July's the month of hospital ro-

tations; on holiday weekends the venerable
                    stay home.
            So when Jason lay blue and inert on the table

and couldn't be made to breathe for three-and-a-
                    quarter hours,
            the staff were too green to let him go.

The household gods have abandoned us to the gods
                    of juris-
            prudence and suburban sprawl. The curve

of new tarmac, the municipal pool,
>> the sky at work
>> on the pock-marked river, fatuous sky,

the park where idling cars, mere yards
>> from the slide
>> and the swingset, deal beautiful oblivion in nickel

bags: the admitting room and its stately drive,
>> possessed
>> of the town's best view.

4.

And what's to become of the three-year-old brother?
>> When Jason was found
>> face down near the dogdish — it takes

just a cupful of water to drown —
>> his brother stood still
>> in the corner and said he was hungry

and said that it wasn't his fault.
>> No fault.
>> The fault's in nature, who will

without system or explanation
>> make permanent
>> havoc of little mistakes. A natural

mistake, the transient ill will we define
　　　　　　as the normal
　　　　　and trust to be inconsequent,

by nature's own abundance soon absorbed.

　　　　　　　5.

Oak wilt, it's called, the new disease.
　　　　　　Like any such
　　　　contagion — hypocrisy in the conference room,

flattery in the halls — it works its mischief mostly
　　　　　　unremarked.
　　　　The men on the links haven't noticed

yet. Their form is good. They're par.
　　　　　　The woman who's
　　　　prospered from hating ideas loves causes

instead. A little shade, a little firewood.
　　　　　　I know
　　　　a stand of oak on which my father's

earthly joy depends. We're slow
　　　　　to cut our losses.

Good News

The hobbled, the halt, the hasten-to-blame-it-on-
        childhood
  crowd, the undermined and over-

their-heads, the hapless,
      the humbugs,
    the hassle-me-nots. The night

before the night my uncle Jens
      saw Jesus
    standing in the hayloft, he —

my uncle Jens, that is — considered
      cashing the whole
    thing in. Bettina gone

the way she had, the boys all gone
      to hell . . .
    The mild flat light of evening lay

like a balm on the fields. But for his heart
      no balm
    in sight. So Jens

gave all his money to the local charis-
                    matic,
          and in exchange his fellow faithful told him

to forgive himself. God's god-
                    forsaken children
          all over the suburbs and the country-

side are dying in the service
                    of a market
          share. Witness

the redhead I used to go to college with,
                    who played
          the trombone and studied Kant and now

performs the laying on of hands somewhere
                    in eastern
          Tennessee. Beneath her touch

quenched sight returns, the myelin sheath
                    repairs
          and lets the wheelchair rust, the cancerous

cat comes purring back to health.
                    But Jens,
          whose otherworldliness imperfectly

cohered, took to driving his pickup
                    off the road,
          in desultory fashion for the most part,

so that cousin Ollie's cornfield took
the brunt
of harm. The hens

ran loose. And Jens, who in his mother's arms
had leapt
for joy and in towheaded youth had leapt

to favor in each tender heart, went weary
to salvation.

2.

Having learned from a well-meaning neighbor
that death
will not have her if Jesus

does first, my three-year-old daughter
is scouring
the visible world for a sign.

The other she's found in abundance —
death on her
dinnerplate, death in the grass —

and drawing just conclusions is beside herself
with fear.
"Most Englishmen,"

the Archbishop said smoothly, "are still residual
                    Christians.
            We still need a clergy for funerals."

The televangelist's plexiglass pulpit,
                    the crystal veil
            of his tears, assure us the soul is

transparent too. No stone can break
                    nor scandal mar
            the radiant flow of video con-

version. Close now, closer
                    than audio
            enhancement, the frictionless

story that washes us clean.
                    Words dis-
            encumbered of contingency,

of history, of doubt. God's
                    wounds,
            they swore, the old ones,

the believers, as now we swear by sex or shit.
            God's wounds,
                which failures of attention made.

For the Taking

And always, the damp blond curls
          on her temples
           and bountifully down to her shoulder blades,

the rich loose curls all summer mixed with sand
          and sweat,
          and the rare, voluptuous double

curve of her nether lip — most children lose
          that ripeness before
          they can talk — and the solemn forehead,

which betokens thought and, alas
          for her, o-
          bedience, and the pure, unmuddied line

of the jaw, and the peeling brown shoulders —
          she was always
          a child of the sun . . . This

was his sweet piece of luck, his
          find,
          his renewable turn-on,

and my brown and golden sister at eight-
          and-a-half
          took to hating her body and cried

in her bath, and this was years,
          my bad uncle did it
      for years, in the back of the car,

in the basement where he kept his guns,
          and we
      who could have saved her, who knew

what it was in the best of times
          to cross
      the bridge of shame, from the body un-

encumbered to the body on the
          block,
      we would be somewhere mowing the lawn

or basting the spareribs right
          outside, and — how
      many times have you heard this? — we

were deaf and blind
          and have
      ever since required of her that she

take care of us, and she has,
          and here's
      the worst, she does it for love.

The Resurrection of the Body

for Caroline Bynum

She must have been thirteen or so, her nascent
        breasts
      just showing above the velcro strap

that held her in her chair.
        Her face
      translucent, beautiful,

as if a cheekbone might directly render
        a tranquil
      heart. And yet

the eyes were all dis-
        quietude.
      The mother with her miraculous

smile, frequent, durable, lifted
        the handkerchief —
      you know the way a woman

will? — her index finger guiding a corner,
        the body of it gathered
      in her dextrous palm — and with

such tenderness wiped the spittle
        pooling
      at her daughter's mouth. The faint

warm smell of lipstick — remember? — freighted
             with love,
        and with that distillate left by fear

when fear's been long outdone by fearful
             fact.
        The mother would give her soul to see

this child lift her head on her own.
             And down
        the hall in orthotics,

I couldn't for the longest time understand
             why the boy
        required a helmet so complexly fitted

and strong — his legs were unused, his arms
             so thin.
        A treadmill, I thought. Or a bicycle maybe, some

bold new stage of therapy anyway, sometimes
             he falls
        and, safe in his helmet, can bravely

set to work again. It wasn't for nothing
             that I was
        so slow. Who cannot read these waiting rooms

has so far — exactly so far — been spared.
             It was only
        while I was driving home,

my daughter in her car seat with her brand-
              new brace,
          that I thought of the boy's rhythmic rocking

and knew. Green light. Yellow. The tide
              of pedestrians
          flush and smooth. And the boy's

poor head against the wall — how could I miss it?
              and what
          does God in his heaven do then? — the boy's

poor head in its bright red helmet knocking —
              listen —
          to be let in.

Bunting

I.

"They're sleeping," said Emma, "they're very
                    tired,"
          as the footage came on again,

child after child in the chalk
                    embrace
          of chemical death. We saw again

the elegant economy with which God
                    sculpts
          the infant face. Not one

not cast in heaven's mold.
                    Not one
          — and how could this be true? — dis-

figured by what brought them here,
                    by death
          throe and the bland assimilations

of the evening news, by lunatic cal-
                    culation
          or malevolence, which launched the gas,

by money, which made it
             and made as well
         the sumptuous ground rhythm

that supplants the children on the screen,
             lures Emma
         full front now and wants her to want

with the whole heart of childhood what
             money
         will buy. The patron's deft

technologies. Our sponsored
             view.
         The cutting-room distillations that can take

our breath away. The man
             in the dust
         and the child in its unearthly

beauty, still in his arms, they're
             Kurds,
         they fell as they ran.

2.

Megan woke up at three last night,
             cold
         and wet and frightened till we made

her warm. We had clean nightclothes.
                    We had
          clean sheets. Plentiful water runs

from the taps. Megan believes that someone's
                    in charge
          here. Megan thinks love

can make you safe. In Vu-
               kovar,
          in our world, in nineteen ninety-one,

they're cutting off limbs with no
                    anesthesia,
          the people have lived in cellars

for eighty-six days. And where there's
               no food
          there's a microphone, and in

the fallen city there's a woman's voice:
               "They have not
          won We do not hate them. We will

not hate them as they hate us."
               But I must
          have misunderstood the first time,

or understood in a clearing somehow, no
               head
          for the trees. Because two

days later I heard the words in another
                    voice, a man's
            voice now, and filtered through trans-

lation: "We do not hate them.
                    They have
            not made us animals."

He, you understand, was on the other side.
                    And both
            of them had the same rumor for proof.

"Unconfirmed," unthinkable,
                    on both sides
            the harrowing goes like this:

We — we're like you — we protected the children,
                    even while the mortars
            made rubble of our town. They

left forty-seven children lying with their
                    throats cut
            on the schoolroom floor.

                    3.

Faster than thought, or the kind that still seems to us
                    human,
            faster than fear or the flaring neuron, upward,

now toward us, now dazzlingly
                    away,
          the missile describes in liquid fire

its deadly, adaptable notion of
                    home
          and makes a sort of conscript of the midnight sky.

Silicon matrix, father
                    land.
          The groundlings in their gas masks need some ground

for hope, but hope's the very substance of dispute,
                    and who
          will draw its boundaries? Here

is the man of seventy-four whose heart quite foolishly
                    stopped,
          though the sirens went off for no reason

that time. Here is the infant
                    who smothered.
          It seems that the valves on the breathing device

can be turned the wrong way. Here
                    is the mother
          who turned them. The missile-seeking missile is

a Patriot, and see how the camera loves it.
                    Heart
          hard-wired to a mobile launcher,

faithlessness keeping the software
true.
No wonder there's confusion on the homefront.

This isn't the shelter we thought we'd
bought,
who've wrapped the child in bunting,

rocked her in the cradle of the state.

Sold

I.

"The delicious part," he said, "is when
      I get her
    to strip the bed. This is after my opening

gambit: she's vacuumed the living room carpet
      with whatever
    she's been using till now,

and I've run the Electrolux over it once and come up
      with a fistful
    of dirt, God's truth — we use

white linen filters and she's watched
      me put
    a new one in. The woman is amazed.

But the part I love is the bedroom:
      she strips
    the linens off the bed, suspicious, you see,

but amused, and I run the hose
      with the curtain
    attachment over the mattress, taking

my time. And when I'm done — are you
      ready for this? —
    the filter bag that was empty and white

when we began is full. Full! Eighty percent
of household dust
is skin cells, I tell her, you shed them

while you sleep. And mites. And here's
the best:
I empty it out right there on the mattress and she

is about to lose it for real. Don't do that! she says
in a horrified
voice, and I say, Why not? It was there

before. Well, you can imagine — she doesn't so much
as wait
until her husband's home from work.

She's written the check out before I can pack."

2.

He was beloved by my friend of the classical
learning,
who slummed and aspired and quoted the ancients

by pinning his heart on a beauty
so frank
and underemployed. I was the wife. The other

wife really, which may be why I so adored
the vacuum cleaner
salesman's talk. This isn't to say I was ever

ill-treated. Never, not once. Just under-
              employed.
        And frightened as one is then

of the world and its regard. When they decided
              to live apart,
        the young one had us to dinner once

on his own, but I had to search through all
              my old
        address books just now to retrieve

his name. He had a gift for wit that worked
              at no
        one else's expense. I haven't

quite caught it, it being a gift I don't
              myself
        possess. Good will resistant to imposture.

My heart was set from then on
              on the kind
        he carried door to door.

Salt

Because she had been told, time and
                again,
          not to swing on the neighbors' high hammock,

and because she had time and again gone
                back, lured
          by the older boys and their dangerous

propulsions, because a child in shock (we
                didn't know
          this yet) can seem sullen or intran-

sigent, and because my father hated his life,
                my sister
          with her collarbone broken was spanked

and sent to bed for the night, to shiver
                through the August
          heat and cry her way through sleep.

And where, while she cried, was the life he
                loved?
          Gone before she was born, of course,

gone with the river-ice stored in sawdust,
                gone with the horses,
          gone with the dogs, gone with Arvid Anacker

up in the barn. 1918. My father was six.
                    His father thought Why
            leave a boy to the women. Ole (like "holy"

without the h, a good Norwegian
                    name)
            Ole had papers to sign, you see,

having served as county JP for years —
                    you
            would have chosen him too, he was salt

of the earth — and Arvid's people needed to cut
                    the body down.
            So Ole took the boy along, my father

that is, and what he hadn't allowed for was
                    how badly
            Arvid had botched it,

even this last job, the man had no luck.
                    His neck
            not having broken, you see, he'd thrashed

for a while, and the northeast wall of the barn —
                    the near wall —
            was everywhere harrows and scythes.

It wasn't — I hope you can understand —
                    the
            blood or the blackening face,

as fearful as those were to a boy, that, forty
                    years later,
          had drowned our days in whiskey and dis-

gust, it was just that the world had no
                    savor left
          once life with the old man was

gone. It's common as dirt, the story
                    of expulsion:
          once in the father's fair

lost field, even the cycles of darkness cohered.
                    Arvid swinging
          in the granular light, Ole as solid

as heartwood, and tall . . . how
                    could a girl
          on her salt-soaked pillow

compete? The banished one in the story
                    measures
          all that might heal him by all

that's been lost. My sister in the hammock
                    by Arvid
          in the barn. I remember

that hammock, a gray and dirty canvas
                    thing,
          I never could make much of it.

But Karen would swing toward the fragrant
              branches, fleshed
        with laughter, giddy with the earth's

sweet pull. Some children are like that,
              I have one
        myself, no wonder we never leave them alone,

we who have no talent for pleasure
              nor use
        for the body but after the fact.

Bad Blood

The question must have been the one
        they all
        ask, How do you feel? And because

these two, the son and the father, had
        nothing
        to say or, more precisely, everything and thus

no words, the camera only lingered for
        the smallest
        part of a minute and then they were gone.

Megan was drinking her apple juice and Emma
        her milk.
        The growths on the boy's pale face

may not have been death's tracks at all —
        they weren't
        the common lesions — but every cell

is death now, those who love him must find
        small res-
        pite in "benign." "Benign" was more

or less what had been judged at law.
        Hemo-
        philiac, lover of blood. And blood

costs money, tainted blood
                    costs money
            to recall. You can guess

what happens to market share once you let
                    the American
            patents in, and screening tests,

homegrown ones, were simply a matter
                    of time.
            In Paris it was already dark. And Justice

in its palace had retired for the night,
                    having found it com-
            prehensible, though dreadful of course,

that ministers of health might have construed the national
                    interest
            as requiring the transmission of incurable

disease. I think I said to Emma when
                    she asked
            that something bad had happened in another

country. Eloquent moral explication,
                    don't you think?
            We dawdled over supper and the tele-

vision news, their father on his way back home,
                    our week's work
            winding down. The pain was someone else's,

I've no claim to it. The pain
                    was someone else's. And the boy.

Mother Ruin

One fall after another. The snow
will oblige. It lies on its back in the drainage
of streetlight. It opens its dress
for the rain. *Old friend. I knew*

we'd be meeting again. Old prompter.
It gives up the bushes, gives up the stairs,
gives up the semblance of order
we've made, the pathways

that signify neighborliness. I am not a learned
iconographer, but I've seen how the patches hold out
under soot. Live long, said my father,
It'll do your mean heart good. Which the rain,

infecting the airborne and earthbound alike
with its news from the yellow sky,
rehearses to obsession: You'll have
your way with your betters at last.

And how the mild hands loosen
their hold. The snow has a mind to simplify,
as I do, I hope, and a body of blessed
amnesia. But always the rain

insinuates, which is death to abide by,
and always the honey-mouthed wind,
till the fastness that made things all of a piece
dissolves.

Creation Myth

(Wheel-thrown stoneware, Richard DeVore)

I.

If the lines are not lovely in two
        dimensions,
           they'll never be lovely in three,

he said. The skirt will not hang right,
        the actress
         will stumble and blur.

And so my friend spent eighteen months
        on the floor
         with her scissors, through headache

and handcramp, recalcitrant muslins, and gavel-
        to-gavel
         coverage of the hearings that traced

a two-bit break-in straight
        to the President's
         heart. Democracy, the hem

of your garment. We had not loved you half
        so well
         had we not loved ineptly.

Till hand could feel and eye behold
                    the seam
            between pattern and in-the-round,

the lip, just blade upon blade of her shears,
                    converting
            clutter to a world of grace.

And then she learned the damasks and silks.
                    And then
            she learned to light them.

                    2.

The child does not walk at a year
                    and a half,
            nor stand without prompting, nor

speak. The kindly professionals plot
                    a curve
            that somehow will not rise as it should.

Please give, say the folding chairs,
                    give,
            say the charts, please give oh give,

says the mother, a sign. The father
                    has not come
            with her, this isn't the business

he meant it to be. Please give, say the child's
                    sweet shoulders,
            a sign, and I will follow, I

will take the world for home.
                    Isn't that
            the story you want? Wheel-thrown,

light-sown, God the potter moves his
                    thumb,
            and what was motion now is

flesh, and still the child
                    does not,
            according to our lights, thrive.

Cortex, medulla, ligament, gut —
                    the least
            conductive membrane with its world

of wit. How dull we are on this scale
                    and behind-
            hand in our praise. Dear

boy, in all your palpable
                    beauty,
            you will have to teach us something we

should long ago have known
                    by heart.

3.

In Norway his training was paint and
                    lathe
            and leafing, artisanal

orders that had no real equiv-
                    alent
            here, where they stole

his luggage and could or would not
                    say
            what it was his mild young

wife was soon to be dead of. But life
                    was harsh
            for so many back then.

He lettered signs and climbed
                    the steeple
            with gold for the cross and once,

for Mrs. Potter-Palmer's third-
                    floor staircase,
            copied a panel of wallpaper lately

plundered from a French chateau.
                    And twice
            on a Sunday (when else

could you paint the rotunda at Marshall
                    Field's?
            this was when people stayed home

after church) twice on a Sunday
   he felt
  the hand of God directly.

Scaffolding broke the first time and he fell
   thirty feet
  to be saved by shattering layers

of glass. Not a soul within ear-
   shot and Lord
  what a wreckage of three-button

gloves. The second time he lost an eye.
   What I
  remember is Oscar Nordby at eighty-

nine, rinsing his eye in an eyecup.
   It must
  have been — don't you think so? — the good

eye, though from this distance I can't
   be sure.
  The one was slightly yellow where the

white should be, and blue of course, and
   the other,
  glass. And always he knew

where the fault had lain.
   Six days
  labor and the seventh day rest,

to honor the father
　　　　　who holds
　　　　a grudge. Eternity, the hem

of your garment. We had
　　　　　not loved you
　　　　half so well had we not noted

what this grief is better than.
　　　　　Do you see
　　　　where the glaze has roughened a bit

like human skin?
　　　　　To honor
　　　　the father who made us.

With Emma at the Ladies-Only Swimming Pond on Hampstead Heath

In payment for those mornings at the mirror while,
        at her
           expense, I'd started my late learning in Applied

French Braids, for all
           the mornings afterward of Hush
        and Just stand still,

to make some small amends for every reg-
           iment-
           ed bathtime and short-shrifted goodnight kiss,

I did as I was told for once,
           gave up
           my map, let Emma lead us through the woods

"by instinct," as the drunkard knew
           the natural
           prince. We had no towels, we had

no "bathing costumes," as the children's novels
           call them here, and I
           am summer's dullest hand at un-

premeditated moves. But when
           the coppice of sheltering boxwood
           disclosed its path and posted

rules, our wonted bows to seemliness seemed
                    poor excuse.
          The ladies in their lumpy variety lay

on their public half-acre of lawn,
                    the water
          lay in dappled shade, while Emma

in her underwear and I
                    in an ill-
          fitting borrowed suit availed us of

the breast stroke and a modified
                    crawl.
          She's eight now. She will rather

die than do this in a year or two
                    and lobbies,
          even as we swim, to be allowed to cut

her hair. I do, dear girl, I will
                    give up
          this honey-colored metric of augmented

thirds, but not (shall we climb
                    on the raft
          for a while?) not yet.

Line Drive Caught
by the Grace of God

Half of America doubtless has the whole
of the infield's peculiar heroics by heart,
this one's way with a fractured forearm,
that one with women and off-season brawls,

the ones who are down to business while their owner
goes to the press. You know them already, the quaint
tight pants, the heft
and repose and adroitness of men

who are kept for a while while they age
with the game. It's time
that parses the other fields too,
one time you squander, next time you hoard,

while around the diamond summer runs
its mortal stall, the torso that thickens,
the face that dismantles its uniform.
And sometimes pure felicity, the length

of a player suspended above the dirt
for a wholly deliberate, perfect catch
for nothing, for New York,
for a million-dollar contract which is nothing now,

for free, for the body
as it plays its deft decline and countless humbling,
deadly jokes, so the body
may once have flattered our purposes.

A man like you or me but for this moment's
delay and the grace of God. My neighbor
goes hungry when the Yankees lose,
his wife's too unhappy to cook,

but supper's a small enough price to pay,
he'd tell you himself, for odds
that make the weeks go by so personal,
so hand in glove.

Target

What is, says the chorus, *this human*
                    desire —
          do you know the part I'm

talking about? *What is this*
                    human
          desire for children? Medea

has just left the stage
                    (*ab-scaena,*
          said my friend, ob-

scene) to brood on her indelible work.
                    His ety-
          mology is false, I've looked it up,

but my friend wasn't thinking
                    of children
          in any case. What

says the mother, for all
                    her books,
          who bathes the newborn child

in the sink, is sick
                    with fear
          for the pulse in the scalp, the foot

still flexed as it was in the womb
          and peeling
      from the amnion. They have no death

in them yet, you see, their very excrement
          is sweet,
      they have no death but what's implied

in the porcelain rim, the drain
          with its food scraps,
      the outlet, the sponge, the thousand

mortal dangers in the kitchen drawer.
          I'd sometimes feel,
      with the child in my arms,

as I've felt looking down on the live
          third rail.
      What is this human desire

for children? They just make a bigger
          target
      for the anger of the gods.

2.

The thing she can't be rid of is that
          no one
      would believe her. Not the uniformed

policeman at the edge of town (and surely
        he knew her?
    the wildest boast of the census

could scarcely have amounted to
        a decent
    row of pews on Christmas Eve),

nor her own forbidding father nor
        good Emma
    at the kitchen sink. Months later

at the jury trial,
        the word
    of a nine-year-old girl would suddenly

count. Late morning
        on the third
    of May in 1929

(the other crash was yet to come),
        no seam
    of comprehension in the ordered world,

no help from the mild
        spring sky,
    my nine-year-old mother ran at last

to the dead girl's house and de-
        livered
    her burden of blight directly. Arrow

unwilling, whoever took pity
        on you?
     The rest replays in borrowed

light: the courtroom in Chicago with its
        unswept floors,
    two girls with their handfuls

of violets. And one leaping one way while the car
        bore down
    and one, my mother, the other.

3.

For those who think, as he did once,
        that in-
    advertent suffering is the worst of it here,

in the range between hating-thy-neighbor
        and destruction
    on a global scale, the middle range,

where people live, the range
        from the hills,
    the journalist describes his con-

versation with a captured Serb.
        The boy —
    the man? — was twenty-two.

I am happy, he said. He must
        have been asked
    what he hoped for or thought

while he lay in the high half-light with his
　　　　　gun,
　　　a sniper in the frozen hills whose

angle on the heart and hearth's acute.
　　　　　I am happy,
　　　he said, *to kill a child crossing*

the street with his mother.
　　　　　Now something
　　　has been altered in the transit

from language to language, this isn't
　　　　　exactly
　　　the way we speak. Offstage,

obscene, the god-from-a-machine
　　　　　at work.
　　　And circuitry whose other name

is "happy": coincident
　　　　　access
　　　of never-on-this-good-green-earth

and ground-from-which-we-start.
　　　　　I am happy
　　　to kill a child crossing the street with his mother.

There is something so fantastic on the mother's face.

Fish Dying on the Third Floor
at Barneys

The clothes are black and unstructured this fall,
    enlivened
      here and there by what appears to be monastic

chic: a crucifix of vaguely Eastern prov-
      enance,
      a cowl. My friend, fresh out of drama school,

explains to me how starkly medieval woolens
      were cut:
      few seams, to spare unraveling, the neck-

notch centered in a single length of cloth.
      High season,
      maiden season at the uptown store, austerity's

a kind of riff in suede and silk. Sumptuous
      charcoals,
      lampblack, slate. And lest the understatement

lose its edge, glaziers have installed
      these fine
      aquaria, within whose bounds, superbly

not for sale, not just at present, swim
      the glories
      of a warmer world. The sun

was always a spendthrift, wasn't it?
                    — cadmium
          yellow, electric blue, and lines that parse

as eat-your-heart-out. Nature's own
                    extravagance,
          and functional, in fins and tails.

But something's wrong. The angelfish
                    near gloves
          and belts is on its side and stalled, grotesquely

heaving at the gills. Says the
                    shopper
          to her boyfriend, "What's it *doing*?"

and she's horrified. Frank
                    dying
          makes a fearful sign of life in here,

it puts the people off their food.
                    Your mother,
          said my father when I teased

her once, and nastily, Your mother always
                    liked
          to save. And who should know

but he and I, who'd lived on her prevenient
                    thrift?
          He didn't say, Uncluttered

is the privilege of the rich these days.
                    Or: In
          a world of built-in obsolescence, saved

means saddled with. He said much later,
                    This
          (I held his hand) This is a bad

business. Nailbeds blue, blue
                    ankles,
          dusky ears. His mucus-

laden lungs and their ungodly labor.
                    Father,
          while there's air to breathe, I mean

to mend my manners.

Bleedthrough

(Helen Frankenthaler, 1969)

I.

As when, in bright daylight, she closes
        her eyes
        but doesn't turn her face away,

or — this is more like it — closes her eyes
        in order
        to take the brightness in,

and the sunstruck coursing of blood through the
        lids
        becomes an exorbitant field to which

there is
        no outside,
        this first plague of being-in-place, this stain

of chemical proneness, leaves so little
        room
        for argument. You'd think

the natural ground of seeing when we see
        no object
        but the self were rage.

2.

My daughter has a trick now of composing
             her face
      and her shoulders and arms in a terrible be-

seeching shape — it all
             takes just
      the blink of an eye — I love

you, Mama, she says, I like
             this food,
      it's good, it's fine, I

can't even taste the burnt part, and she means
             Don't rain
      down fire again. She's nine.

And every penitent reparation — Do you like
             me, reader?
      Do you like me sorry now? — ensnares

her more and makes her shoulder
             more
      of this im-

partible estate. It seemed like
             Mars
      to me when I was young, that other

3.

world of women with its four fleshed walls
        of love.
        My mother, who can turn the most unlikely

raw materials to gladness, used
        to call
        her monthly blood "the curse." I

know, I know, our arsenal of pills
        is new,
        our tampons and detergents, all

our euphemizing gear; the body
        in even its
        flourishing seethes and cramps. When the

painter, for example, looks for
        leverage
        on a metaphor, nine-

tenths of her labor is in-the-flesh. The wash
        of acrylic,
        the retinal flare: we say

that the surfeited pigment "bleeds." And
        every
        counter-argument — the margin of shoreline,

the margin of black, the four-
                    fold
            margin she's stretched the canvas to com-

prehend — undoes itself a little in its straining after
                    emphasis.
            I can tell, says my daughter, the difference between

                    4.

the morning light and light at the end
                    of the day.
            And from room to room in the crowded

museum she blazons her facility. That's night. That's
                    not. That's
            Sunset Corner, says the plaque. As though

the vaults of fire had found their
                    boundary
            in an act of wit, or California's amplitude

in glib suburban pavement. Or have I
                    missed
            the point again? Outflanking

the painter's luxuriant brushwork
                    (maybe
            I've loved this grief too well) is

something more quotidian and harder
                won.
        The fretted cloth on the third or fourth rinsing goes

yellow, goes brown, the young
                girl's hands
          — she's just pubescent — ache

with cold. Some parts
                (the red's
          bare memory now) were never bad. The sound

of the water, for instance, the smell,
                the rim
          of the stain that's last to go.

Luke 17:32

Remember, he said, *Lot's wife,* which is
        as much
        as to say, Look back, and at your peril,

on the rigors of the backward look.
        Two men
        in a bed and the one

shall be taken, the other left. Two daughters
        and their father's
        seed. How is it in this second

world, the one where we start over, that
        we still
        can't get the story right? Who

cannot read shall not
        be saved.
        Who comes down from the housetop

to gather his things for flight shall be
        lost.
        But where? said the twelve.

Wherever the body is, there,
        said the one.
      And there (but whose?) the chapter

ends, the body turned to salt again.

2.
(Cuylerville, New York)

Three months before the mine caved in,
        the miner's wife
      sent letters to the Post-Dispatch:

The underground ceilings, she wrote, have cracked;
        they're drilling
      at the salt supports that keep the chambers

stable. But ice was bad that winter and the pay
        was good.
      The midnight blasting barely

set our sleep on edge until, just shy
        of dawn
      one night, the roar

beneath the village and its salted roads
        convinced us
      we were done for. *Two women*

shall be grinding and the one
      shall be taken,
   the other left. And look at us now.

Sinkholes big as parking lots, the wells
      sucked dry,
   beds that were once a Devonian sea

dissolving in the aquifer.
      You've heard
   what they called it, the prophets of doom

and eco-disaster, when word
      of the new-style
   mining got out? They called it "pillar robbing,"

and (we're all adept at hindsight now) they got
      it right.
   Two men in a field; the one

shall be taken, the other . . . The other
      thing left
   to contemplate is fire and brimstone, honest to

God: hydrogen sulfide burning off for
      twenty-one
   months, you've never smelled the like of it.

3.

The old law left some haggling room (If you
                     find there ten
          who are righteous will you stay your hand?) and Lot

leaned hard on his angels.
                     I cannot
          escape to the mountain, he told them. *Let*

me escape to the city nearby, it is
                     a little
          one. But the woman *Is it not*

looked back *a little one?* Little enough.
                     Now which
          strikes you as tempting fate?

4.

"For Olaf," on the flyleaf, "Merry Christmas,
                     1943,"
          and off to Guam, whose damps

wreaked all this havoc with the leather
                     spine.
          Shipped out by way of Oakland, where

a blue-eyed sailor lately off the
                     farm
          encountered passes of a whole new sort. I doubt

he did much reading. On
                        the jungle's
            edge, once night set in, they'd stare

through the tropical downpour at a makeshift
                        screen: Miss
            Carole Lombard take

us home. Perimeter fan club of native
                        Chamorros
            and, just beyond the barbed-wire fence,

the groundling Japanese ("We caught
                        one in
            the chow line once"), who crept back

to the trees when the credits came on.
                        By the light
            of a lab in New Mexican desert *One*

shall be Admiral *one shall be* Nimitz
            take us home.

                        5.

Will it be in our lifetime? they wanted
                        to know,
            and who but the most embarrassed

of masters could blame them? *Does he*
                        thank
            the servant because he served?

Intractable meantime (neither
              would you),
        embarrassment makes us cruel.

For forty years, my father talked so much
              about dying,
        talked loud in his whiskey, talked matter-of-

fact in his woods, and always with
              such flat
        satisfaction, you'd think he was sizing up acreage

and yield. I thought he'd be impatient with our
              salt
        farewells. But he was simply ready.

The Woman Who Died
in Her Sleep

Jeffrey Silverthorne, photographer

I.

Not whipstitch nor blindstitch
          nor any
               sort of basting stitch I recognize, black

cordage, really, piercing its way from pubis
          to breast-
              bone — why not? — up to shoulder, the coroner's

question flatly left
          to the body's
             implacable gray. The part

in her hair is jagged too.
          Amazing
             what the flesh can make of all this in-

terruption. You've
          gathered
             that she's beautiful.

2.

When Megan chose the fifteenth-century sculpture
                    rooms, I
          realized with some chagrin

she hadn't any notion who these
                    people
          were. The one in blue,

I said, is Mary, and the one
                    she's
          holding in her lap . . . till Megan

got the gist of it. And here,
                    I said,
          is how you'll know him when they take

him down: five wounds. But my five-
                    year-old
          daughter saw six. Have I

told you — do you know for yourself — how the
                    sweetness
          of creation may be summed up in the lightfall

on a young girl's cheek? The wound
                    she hadn't yet
          learned to ignore, the mortal one, was where

the child had once been joined
                    to something else.

3.

She'd had worse news, the pale one, she'd felt terror
        sink
      its claw and hold, and never

had she lapsed into so lumpish
        a cliché.
      The bright young surgeon showed

her how to read the stark trans-
        parency,
      the telltale script of cells

gone wrong. And like some dull
        beginner
      she began to lose the edge of things

and had to sit (I'm
        sorry),
      had to drink some water (I'm

not like this, I can hear). The
        punishment
      for self-absorbed, she thought, is self-

absorbed. And all this black periphery
        is chiefly
      lack of blood flow to the

brain. Poor brain. It's body too.
        Is this,
      this old embarrassment, the way I'll know?

4.

The woman in the photograph is
                lying
        on a pallet made of wood. And though

her abdomen appears to have been
                packed
        again in haste and though the breast

is badly sewn,
                her hips
        are smooth parentheses, her cheekbones

high, her lovely arms disposed as though
                in languor
        or luxurious thought. They took

my mother's teeth away — they had
                to, I can
        understand — the morphine I'd bullied them

into providing was meager
                and frequently
        late. And so my mother's face was not

the face I knew. But, reader,
                her
        fine forehead was a blessing on the place.

The lesson, though I'm clumsy here, has something
                to do

5.

with beauty and use.

The sculptors whose grammar my Megan
recites —
a hole in each hand, a hole

in each foot, an entry
point
beneath the breast — believed we get our

bodies back. And all the urgent calculus
that death
can found and dis-

solution expedite was lavished in that era
on this one
account:

What of the fingernails? What
of the hair?
The menses? The milk? The proud-

flesh worn for heaven's sake?
Who'd want,
you see, the body oblivious? — body

on which the stern salt tide
had left
no mark? When Megan

hadn't yet been born — two months to go —
        my ankles swelled
    and doubled over every pair of shoes

I wore. Unseemliness, you seem
        to have some
    thing in mind. Imagine,

said the people once:
        a world
    where nothing is thrown away.

Linda Gregerson is the author of a previous book of poetry, *Fire in the Conservatory.* Her awards include the Levinson Prize from *Poetry* magazine, the Consuelo Ford Award from the Poetry Society of America, the Isabel MacCaffrey Award from the Spenser Society of America, and numerous grants and fellowships. Gregerson was for two years an actress in Herbert Blau's experimental theater company, Kraken, and for six years a staff editor in poetry at *The Atlantic Monthly.* She is a noted critic of contemporary American poetry and publishes widely on Renaissance literature. Gregerson is also the author of a book of criticism, *The Reformation of the Subject: Spenser, Milton, and the English Protestant Epic* (Cambridge University Press). She teaches at the University of Michigan and lives in Ann Arbor with her husband and two daughters.